I0838062

Table of Contents

Intro to KKK..2
Timeline – Part 1..14
Intro to CIA...24
Timeline – Part 2..46
Wrapping It Up..74
References...78

Intro to KKK

…..

War is funny.

I suppose it could be said that a good chunk of someone's personality is formed by which war they have… an affinity for.

…..

I'm WWI.

I grant you, this wasn't the case while growing up.

This happened… in stages, as the world I grew up in more or less crumbled away.

It just seemed the most relevant.

While starting to connect events onto some kind of timeline, I had to determine what kind of context I was going to put this in. - At first I thought U.S. presidents was the obvious choose, but that didn't really work. Then I started to think U.S. wars might be better. But what's a U.S. war?

One website listed the major conflicts as follows: American Revolution / War of 1812 / Mexican-American War / Civil War / Spanish-American War / WWI / WWII / Korean War / Vietnam War / Gulf War /War in Afghanistan / Iraq War

(White, n.d.)

…..

Okay… I guess.

…..

Double checked with Wiki…

HOLY… cow!

Yes! This was it…

American Revolutionary War (1775–1783), Cherokee–American wars (1776–1795) Part of the American Indian Wars, Northwest Indian War (1785–1793) Part of the American Indian Wars, Quasi-War (1798–1800), First Barbary War (1801–1805) Part of the Barbary Wars, Tecumseh's War (1810–1813) Part of the American Indian Wars and the War of 1812, War of 1812 (1812–1815), Creek War
(1813–1814) Part of the American Indian Wars and the War of 1812, Second Barbary War (1815) Part of the Barbary Wars, First Seminole War (1817–1818) Part of the Seminole Wars and the American Indian Wars…

TELL ME YOU DON'T SEE A CHARGING CAVALRY ON THE HORIZON!

Arikara War (1823) Part of the American Indian Wars, Winnebago War (1827) Part of the American Indian Wars, Black Hawk War (1832) Part of the American Indian Wars, Texas Revolution (1835–1836), Second Seminole War (1835–1842) Part of the Seminole Wars and the American Indian Wars, Texas Comanche Wars (1836–1875) Part of the Texas–Indian wars and the American Indian Wars, Aroostook War (1838–1839), Mexican–American War (1846–1848), Cayuse War (1847–1855) Part of the American Indian Wars, Apache Wars (1849–1924) Part of the Texas–Indian wars and the American Indian Wars, Navajo Wars (1849–1866) Part of the American Indian Wars, Bleeding Kansas (1854–1861), Puget Sound War (1855–1856) Part of the American Indian Wars, Rogue River Wars

(1855–1856), Third Seminole War (1855–1858) Part of the
Seminole Wars and the American Indian Wars, Yakima War
(1855–1858) Part of the American Indian Wars, Second Opium
War (1856–1859) Part of the Opium Wars, Utah War (1857–1858)
Part of the Mormon wars, Reform War
(1858–1866), Pig War (1859), John Brown's Raid on Harpers
Ferry (1859) Part of pre-Civil War conflicts, First and Second
Cortina War (1859–1861), Paiute War (1860) Part of the
American Indian Wars, American Civil War (1861–1865)

("List of wars involving the United States," 2023)

OKAY, HERE WE GO!

It's really quite amazing. Just reading down the list of all the wars
the U.S. has been involved in…

You really do end up feeling like a Southerner. – Someone that
just exists in an environment with no other industry… but war.

This is, of course, assuming you're not a wealthy plantation
owner.

…..

I'm sure Southern society was more dynamic than I'm giving it
credit for, but the old stereotype really holds sway.

There's a lot of history on this timeline.

Pretty small range, as far as history goes, but it's packed solid.

…..

Big deal.

You probably weren't even born when a lot of this stuff happened.

Or maybe you were too young to even know it was happening.

Same here.

So why bother?

America's changed quite a lot.

Or has it?

Either way, the way we're living through it is *certainly* changing.

For everyone.

Everywhere.

Whatever significance this timeline may or may not have, the words used to mark the events listed on it fall short. – Tragically so.

In an attempt to give substance to these words, I've added some links to online sources that have either documented these events or display works by those inspired by them. (If you're old-schooling it with the paperback edition of this manuscript, please go to YouTube and refer to the titles I've included just above the links.)

Don't be thrown by the fact that a good portion of them are just reflections of how this culture commemorates such things, i. e., segments of old television shows and movies.

As a matter of fact, the use of fiction to commemorate a culture is a long standing practice. – The Daughter's of the Confederacy used it to great advantage.

I'm not sure how much they're responsible for what we take as South culture, but for quite some time (probably not), the cultivation of a Southern gentleman usually meant attending a military academy during some point in a young man's live.

In commemoration of this, I invite you to experience this myth (or not myth) by following the first of many links to the hallowed halls of that *still* famous (or not) Southern institution, THE CITADEL…

"…The next day, we marched down to Marion Square, and we renewed our oath…"

Rite of Passage | Our Mighty Citadel
https://www.youtube.com/watch?v=YYCgPCsnowc

(The Citadel, 2019, 1:44)

You still there?

You know… some of this stuff isn't going to be easy to watch.

I don't think it's supposed to be.

…..

I think it's meant to be *"enlightening"*… whatever *that* means.

Tell you what, let's start slow.

I call the next few links, "A Taste of the South".

"...we're not going to take them and push them off somewhere
just because we could do it…"

His Smile Is Fake. Watch Southerners Tell Him Segregation Was
Better For Black Americans.
https://www.youtube.com/watch?v=6gX6WIEzB08

(Hoffman, 2018, 0:10)

"Today, I have stood where once Jefferson Davis stood, and took an oath to my people..."

George Wallace "Segregation Forever" Speech
https://www.youtube.com/watch?v=6C-kBVggFrs

(TastySpaceApple, 2014)

Do You Believe This Town

Roy Clark - Do You Believe This Town
https://www.youtube.com/watch?v=C0ceQumLxYY
(Baumruk, 2012)

Too dated?

Well, I grew up in the 70's. So, although these ideas *were* foreign to me, I still understood that such people existed. And, like you, that enlightenment usually came by way of pop culture.

…..

As a matter of fact, let's just get this out of the way…

I accessed this video clip on December 12, 2022. But for some reason, I can no longer find a trace of this episode anywhere. - Even Amazon removed it from its site.

"...He only wrote one dumb letter! - Yeah, but it was a very dangerous and subversion letter, Arch…"

All in the Family Season 8 Episode 11: Archie and the KKK - Part 2

"…Klansmen don't apologize to their kind."

The Jeffersons | Sorry, Wrong Meeting | Season 7 Episode 14
Full Episode | The Norman Lear Effect
https://www.youtube.com/watch?v=cP-Fs2EashA

(The Norman Lear Effect, 2022, 8:57)

"...David Duke, who was a white supremist, who scared the heck
out of everybody when he ran for public office and did better

than was expected, was an unusual character. He had a kind of schoolboy appearance about him. He was a rather nice looking guy. You know, nothing offensive about him. And then out comes this rhetoric..."
Phil Donahue on interviewing David Duke - EMMYTVLEGENDS.ORG
https://www.youtube.com/watch?v=AnRjtg37two

(FoundationINTERVIEWS, 2016)

"...they were smart enough to know to leave town before the sun went down."

Oprah Visits a County Where No Black Person Had Lived for 75 Years | The Oprah Winfrey Show | OWN
https://www.youtube.com/watch?v=WErjPmFulQ0
(OWN, 2015, 3:59)

Okay, all that was old stuff. Now, the next video is *definitely* old *BUT* historical… so… yeah, it's supposed to be old… Oh, heads-up, this one's an hour long.

"The South was in turmoil…"

Segregation and the South - Fund for the Republic Records
https://www.youtube.com/watch?v=tfgQdCld3Fg

(princetonacademics, 2014, 9:55)

Let's not leave Hollywood out of it…

"…Outsiders have come into Jessup County, Mississippi. And

they've been people of low morality. Unhygienic. And their presence here has provoked a lot of people. So the court understands, without condoning them, mind you, that the crimes to which you men have pled guilty were, to some extent at least, provoked by these outside influences…"

Mississippi Burning 1988 part 9 (Full Movie)
https://www.youtube.com/watch?v=plH2xKFKapE

(Doc Holiday, 2022, 4:32)

"You know, if I were a negro, I'd probably think the same way they do." – "If you were a negro, nobody would give a damn what you thought."

Mississippi Burning 1988 part 9 (Full Movie)
https://www.youtube.com/watch?v=plH2xKFKapE

(Doc Holiday, 2022, 6:54)

Okay, that's the KKK setup.

I'll meet you somewhere in the middle for the CIA stuff.

Timeline – Part 1

… American Civil War (1861–1865)

This is not deep diving boys and girls.

As a matter of fact, I would venture to use the term "Pop Culture".

I DuckDuckGo'ed this and came up with Wikipedia, Britannica, National Geographic, and History.com.

Yeah, there were a few more, but I'm okay with these.

And, no, I didn't bother venturing beyond the first page.

Now, back to my pop culture…

American Civil War

"The American Civil War (April 12, 1861 – May 26, 1865; also known by other names) was a civil war in the United States. It was fought between the Union ("the North") and the Confederacy ("the South"), the latter formed by states that had seceded. The central cause of the war was the dispute over whether slavery would be permitted to expand into the western territories, leading to more slave states, or be prevented from doing so, which was widely believed would place slavery on a course of ultimate extinction…"

("American Civil War," 2023)

1861

Yavapai Wars (1861–1875) Part of the American Indian Wars, Dakota War of 1862 (1862) Part of the American Indian Wars, Colorado War (1863–1865) Part of the American Indian Wars, Snake War (1864–1868) Part of the American Indian Wars, Powder River War (1865) Part of the American Indian Wars

("List of wars involving the United States," 2023)

KKK

"… The first Klan was established in the wake of the American Civil War and was a defining organization of the Reconstruction era. Organized in numerous chapters across the Southern United States, federal law enforcement suppressed it around 1871. It sought to overthrow the Republican state governments in the South, especially by using voter intimidation and targeted violence against African-American leaders. Each chapter was autonomous and highly secretive about membership and plans. Members made their own, often colorful, costumes: robes, masks and conical hats, designed to be terrifying and to hide their identities…"

("Ku Klux Klan," 2023)

"… The 19th-century Klan reached its peak between 1868 and 1870. A potent force, it was largely responsible for the restoration of white rule in North Carolina, Tennessee, and Georgia. But Forrest ordered it disbanded in 1869, largely as a result of the group's excessive violence. Local branches remained active for a time, however, prompting Congress to pass the Force Act in 1870 and the Ku Klux Klan Act in 1871… In United States v. Harris in 1882, the Supreme Court declared the Ku Klux Klan Act unconstitutional, but by that time the Klan had practically disappeared. It disappeared because its original objective—the restoration of white supremacy throughout the South—had been largely achieved during the 1870s. The need for a secret antiblack organization diminished accordingly…"

("Ku Klux Klan hate organization, United States," n.d.)

"… Late in 1865, just after the United States Civil War ended, the Ku Klux Klan (KKK) was founded. The Klan, a secret organization that used terror tactics to target newly freed African Americans, attracted defeated Confederates who resented the changes of Reconstruction. Under the cloak of darkness and in disguise, the KKK worked to enforce white supremacy as the political and social order of the South…"

("The Ku Klux Klan," 2022)

"In Pulaski, Tennessee, a group of Confederate veterans convenes to form a secret society that they christen the "Ku Klux Klan." The KKK rapidly grew from a secret social fraternity to a paramilitary force bent on reversing the federal government's progressive Reconstruction era-activities in the South, especially policies that elevated the rights of the local Black population…"

("KKK founded," 2019)

(Public Domain Images KKK)

1866

Red Cloud's War (1866–1868) Part of the American Indian Wars, Formosa Expedition (1867), Comanche Campaign (1867–1875) Part of the American Indian Wars, United States expedition to Korea (1871), Modoc War (1872–1873) Part of the American Indian Wars, Red River War
(1874–1875) Part of the American Indian Wars, Las Cuevas War (1875), Great Sioux War of 1876
(1876–1877) Part of the American Indian Wars, Buffalo Hunters' War (1876–1877) Part of the American Indian Wars, Nez Perce War (1877) Part of the American Indian Wars, Bannock War (1878) Part of the American Indian Wars, Cheyenne War (1878–1879) Part of the American Indian Wars, Sheepeater Indian War (1879) Part of the American Indian Wars, Victorio's War (1879–1880) Part of the American Indian Wars, White River War (1879)

Part of the American Indian Wars, Egyptian Expedition (1882)
Part of the Anglo-Egyptian War, Crow War (1887) Part of the
American Indian Wars, Ghost Dance War (1890–1891) Part of the
American Indian Wars, Bering Sea Anti-Poaching Operations
(1891), Garza War (1891–1893), Yaqui Wars (1896–1918) Part of
the American Indian Wars, Second Samoan Civil War (1898–
1899)

("List of wars involving the United States," 2023)

The Spanish–American War

"The Spanish–American War (April 21 – August 13, 1898) was a
period of armed conflict between Spain and the United States.
Hostilities began in the aftermath of the internal explosion of USS
Maine in Havana Harbor in Cuba, leading to United States
intervention in the Cuban War of Independence. The war led to
the United States emerging predominant in the Caribbean region,
and resulted in U.S. acquisition of Spain's Pacific possessions. It
led to United States involvement in the Philippine Revolution and
later to the Philippine–American War..."

("Spanish–American War," 2023)

1899

Philippine–American War (1899–1902), Moro Rebellion (1899–
1913), Boxer Rebellion (1899–1901)

("List of wars involving the United States," 2023)

20th-Century

Crazy Snake's War (1909) Part of the American Indian Wars, Mexican Border War (1910–1919) Part of the Mexican Revolution, Little Race War (1912) Part of the Banana Wars, United States occupation of Nicaragua (1912–1933) Part of the Banana Wars, Bluff War (1914–1915) Part of the American Indian Wars

("List of wars involving the United States," 2023)

World War I

"… Prior to 1914, the European great powers were divided between the Triple Entente (comprising France, Russia, and Britain) and the Triple Alliance (containing Germany, Austria-Hungary, and Italy). Tensions in the Balkans came to a head on 28 June 1914, following the assassination of Archduke Franz Ferdinand of Austria-Hungary by Gavrilo Princip, a Bosnian Serb. Austria-Hungary blamed Serbia, which led to the July Crisis, an unsuccessful attempt to avoid conflict through diplomacy. On 28 July 1914, Austria-Hungary declared war on Serbia, while Russia came to the latter's defence. By the 4th of August, Germany, France, and Britain (along with their respective colonies) were also drawn into the war. In November 1914, the Ottoman Empire, Germany, and Austria-Hungary formed the Central Powers, and on 26 April 1915, Italy joined Britain, France, Russia, and Serbia as the Allies of World War I…"

("World War I," 2023)

1914

United States occupation of Veracruz (1914) Part of the Mexican Revolution, United States occupation of Haiti (1915–1934) Part of the Banana Wars

("List of wars involving the United States," 2023)

KKK

"… The second Klan started in 1915 as a small group in Georgia. It grew after 1920 and flourished nationwide in the early and mid-1920s, including urban areas of the Midwest and West. Taking inspiration from D. W. Griffith's 1915 silent film The Birth of a Nation, which mythologized the founding of the first Klan, it employed marketing techniques and a popular fraternal organization structure. Rooted in local Protestant communities, it sought to maintain white supremacy, often took a pro-Prohibition and pro-compulsory public education[63][64][65] stance, and it opposed Jews, while also stressing its opposition to the alleged political power of the pope and the Catholic Church. This second Klan flourished both in the south and northern states; it was funded by initiation fees and selling its members a standard white costume. The chapters did not have dues. It used K-words which were similar to those used by the first Klan, while adding cross

burnings and mass parades to intimidate others. It rapidly
declined in the latter half of the 1920s…”

(“Ku Klux Klan,” 2023)

“… The 20th-century Klan had its roots more directly in the
American nativist tradition. It was organized in 1915 near Atlanta,
Georgia, by Col. William J. Simmons, a preacher and promoter of
fraternal orders who had been inspired by Thomas Dixon's book
The Clansman (1905) and D.W. Griffith's film The Birth of a
Nation (1915). The new organization remained small until
Edward Y. Clarke and Elizabeth Tyler brought to it their talents as
publicity agents and fund raisers. The revived Klan was fueled
partly by patriotism and partly by a romantic nostalgia for the old
South, but, more importantly, it expressed the defensive reaction
of white Protestants in small-town America who felt threatened
by the Bolshevik revolution in Russia and by the large-scale
immigration of the previous decades that had changed the ethnic
character of American society…”

(Wallenfeldt, n.d.)

“… The Klan would be revived in the early 20th century with its
falsely heroic portrayal in The Birth of a Nation film. The influx
of Catholic and Jewish immigrants from Eastern Europe offered a
new target for the Klan's prejudice.”

(“The Ku Klux Klan | National Geographic Society,” 2022)

“… In 1915, white Protestant nativists organized a revival of the
Ku Klux Klan near Atlanta, Georgia, inspired by their romantic
view of the Old South as well as Thomas Dixon's 1905 book
“The Clansman” and D.W. Griffith's 1915 film ‘Birth of a
Nation.’

This second generation of the Klan was not only anti-Black but also took a stand against Roman Catholics, Jews, foreigners and organized labor. It was fueled by growing hostility to the surge in immigration that America experienced in the early 20th century along with fears of communist revolution akin to the Bolshevik triumph in Russia in 1917. The organization took as its symbol a burning cross and held rallies, parades and marches around the country. At its peak in the 1920s, Klan membership exceeded 4 million people nationwide…"

("Ku Klux Klan," 2022)

Public Domain – NY Public Library Digital Collection

(Public Domain - Washington D.C. 1926)

1916

United States occupation of the Dominican Republic (1916–1924) Part of the Banana Wars, World War I (1917–1918), Russian Civil War (1918–1920), Posey War (1923) Part of the American Indian Wars

("List of wars involving the United States," 2023)

KKK

The conviction of D. C. Stephenson, Grand Dragon of the Indiana Klan in 1925 for the murder of Madge Oberholtzer, a white schoolteacher, led to the decline of the Indiana Klan.

("Ku Klux Klan," 2023)

"… The Great Depression in the 1930s depleted the Klan's membership ranks…"

("Ku Klux Klan," 2022)

Intro to CIA

<u>WHAT</u> – <u>A</u> – <u>MESS!</u>

For an organization that's supposed to be clandestine, it certainly does get around.

Talk about cocky.

I ended up inserting the KKK bits into the *CIA...*

Well, I can't really say *bits*.

If you've been paying attention, you might have noticed that sometimes I'll make a point of inserting the exact year, while at other times I'll just put things in chronological order.

I'm doing this just to clarify where we're at when things start piling up on each other.

If you've a history buff, you might also have noticed the absence of any reference to the FBI.

.....

In all honesty, boys and girls… this isn't intended for a domestic audience. – The world's got enough
problems.

Too simplistic for a global audience?

Well, if that's the case, let's just say this work is intended for the American expat community.

So… what's the CIA?

Growing up in Miami, Florida, to me the CIA was Bay of Pigs and Doonesbury.

…..

Well… it's certainly become more substantial now…

Miami Before Miami Vice

"They call him Flipper, Flipper, faster than lighting…"

300 Feet Below | Full Episode S01E01 | Flipper
https://www.youtube.com/watch?v=cuKslEBQdSg

(TV Rerun Club by MGM, 2022, 3:04)

But I digress…

"The Central Intelligence Agency known informally as the Agency and historically as the Company, is a civilian foreign intelligence service of the federal government of the United States, officially tasked with gathering, processing, and analyzing national security information from around the world, primarily through the use of human intelligence (HUMINT) and performing covert actions…"

("Central Intelligence Agency," 2023)

"The CIA, or Central Intelligence Agency, is the U.S. government agency tasked primarily with gathering intelligence and international security information from foreign countries…"

("CIA," 2018)

"Central Intelligence Agency (CIA), principal foreign intelligence and counterintelligence agency of the U.S. government…"

(Pringle, 2022)

Pulling up information about the CIA…

Yeah, well…

This time I *did* have to go beyond the first page:

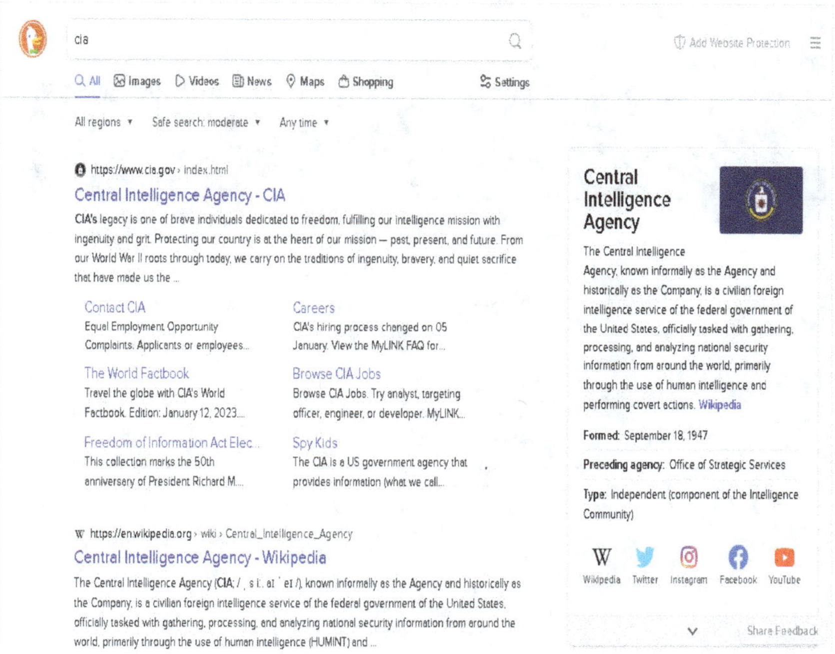

CIA's legacy is one of brave individuals dedicated to freedom, fulfilling our intelligence mission with ingenuity and grit. Protecting our country is at the heart of our mission — past, present, and future. From our World War II roots through today, we carry on the traditions of ingenuity, bravery, and quiet sacrifice that have made us the …

https://www.cia.gov › stories › news

News - CIA - Central Intelligence Agency

CIA Unveils Its First Ever Federal Lab. The Central Intelligence Agency launched **CIA** Labs, a federal laboratory and in-house research and development arm for **CIA** to drive science and technology breakthroughs for tomorrow's intelligence challenges.

Recent News

CIA chief makes rare visit to Libya

Reuters | 2d

Morgan Freeman Joins Taylor Sheridan's CIA Drama 'Lioness' at Paramount+

YAHOO!News | 2d

Morgan Freeman Joins Star-Studded Cast of New Paramount+ CIA Drama Lioness

YAHOO!News | 2d

More News →

Are these links helpful? Yes   No

https://www.cia.gov › careers › index-html

Careers - CIA - Central Intelligence Agency

Why Work at **CIA**? We are an Agency defined by our mission, values, and people. Together, we accomplish what others cannot accomplish and go where others cannot go. When you're a part of the Nation's premier intelligence agency, your opportunities for personal and professional growth are boundless. Get Details.

Morgan Freeman Joins Star-Studded Cast of New Paramount+ CIA Drama Lioness

This one's a twofer…

https://www.cia.gov › stories › news

News - CIA - Central Intelligence Agency

CIA Unveils Its First Ever Federal Lab. The Central Intelligence Agency launched **CIA** Labs, a federal laboratory and in-house research and development arm for **CIA** to drive science and technology breakthroughs for tomorrow's intelligence challenges.

Recent News

CIA chief makes rare visit to Libya

Reuters | 2d

Morgan Freeman Joins Taylor Sheridan's CIA Drama 'Lioness' at Paramount+

YAHOO!News | 2d

Morgan Freeman Joins Star-Studded Cast of New Paramount+ CIA Drama Lioness

YAHOO!News | 2d

More News →

Are these links helpful? Yes   No

https://www.cia.gov › careers › index-html

Careers - CIA - Central Intelligence Agency

Why Work at **CIA**? We are an Agency defined by our mission, values, and people. Together, we accomplish what others cannot accomplish and go where others cannot go. When you're a part of the Nation's premier intelligence agency, your opportunities for personal and professional growth are boundless. Get Details.

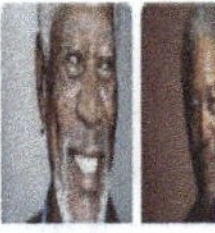

Careers - CIA - Central Intelligence Agency

Why Work at **CIA**? We are an Agency defined by our mission, values, and people. Together, we accomplish what others cannot accomplish and go where others cannot go. When you're a part of the Nation's premier intelligence agency, your opportunities for personal and professional growth are boundless. Get Details.

https://www.usa.gov › federal-agencies › central-intelligence-agency

Central Intelligence Agency | USAGov

Central Intelligence Agency. The Central Intelligence Agency (**CIA**) collects, evaluates, and disseminates vital information on economic, military, political, scientific, and other developments abroad to safeguard national security.

https://247wallst.com › special-report › 2023 › 01 › 14 › cia-scandals-and-outrageous-operations

16 of the Most Outrageous Operations in CIA History

1 day ago · To find scandals involving the **CIA** and contentious operations of the spy agency, 24/7 Wall St. poured over historical and media sources as well as declassified Senate, **CIA**, and other government ...

https://www.intelligence.gov › how-the-ic-works › our-organizations › 411-cia

INTEL - Central Intelligence Agency

Central Intelligence Agency. The Central Intelligence Agency (**CIA**) was created in 1947 with the signing of the National Security Act by President Harry S. Truman. The Director of the Central Intelligence Agency (DCIA) serves as the head of the **CIA** and reports to the Director of National Intelligence. The **CIA** assists the DCIA in carrying out the ...

https://abcnews.go.com › International › wireStory › cia-chief-rare-visit-libya-meets-tripoli-based-9...

CIA chief in rare visit to Libya, meets Tripoli-based PM

3 days ago · TRIPOLI, Libya -- The **CIA** chief has met with one of Libya's rival prime ministers, the government in the country's capital of Tripoli said Thursday. It was a rare visit by a senior U.S. official ...

https://www.atlasobscura.com › articles › cia-cold-war-pigeon-spies

When the CIA Spied on American Citizens—Using Pigeons

4 days ago · Cher Ami, a black checker pigeon, earned his fame carrying messages for the American military during World War I. The pigeons recruited by the **CIA** during the Cold War were trained to

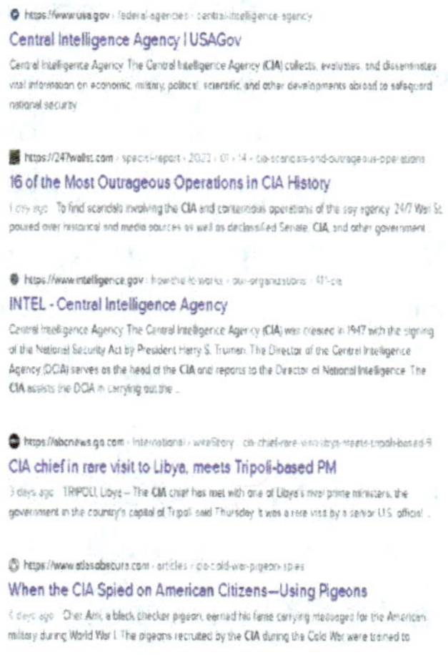

https://www.usa.gov › federal-agencies › central-intelligence-agency

Central Intelligence Agency | USAGov

Central Intelligence Agency. The Central Intelligence Agency (CIA) collects, evaluates, and disseminates vital information on economic, military, political, scientific, and other developments abroad to safeguard national security.

https://247wallst.com › special-report › 2023 › 01 › 14 › cia-scandals-and-outrageous-operations

16 of the Most Outrageous Operations in CIA History

1 day ago · To find scandals involving the CIA and contentious operations of the spy agency, 24/7 Wall St. poured over historical and media sources as well as declassified Senate, CIA, and other government ...

https://www.intelligence.gov › how-the-ic-works › our-organizations › 411-cia

INTEL - Central Intelligence Agency

Central Intelligence Agency. The Central Intelligence Agency (CIA) was created in 1947 with the signing of the National Security Act by President Harry S. Truman. The Director of the Central Intelligence Agency (DCIA) serves as the head of the CIA and reports to the Director of National Intelligence. The CIA assists the DCIA in carrying out the ...

https://abcnews.go.com › International › wireStory › cia-chief-rare-visit-libya-meets-tripoli-based-9...

CIA chief in rare visit to Libya, meets Tripoli-based PM

3 days ago · TRIPOLI, Libya -- The CIA chief has met with one of Libya's rival prime ministers, the government in the country's capital of Tripoli said Thursday. It was a rare visit by a senior U.S. official ...

https://www.atlasobscura.com › articles › cia-cold-war-pigeon-spies

When the CIA Spied on American Citizens—Using Pigeons

4 days ago · Cher Ami, a black checker pigeon, earned his fame carrying messages for the American military during World War I. The pigeons recruited by the CIA during the Cold War were trained to

16 of the Most Outrageous Operations in CIA History

1 day ago To find scandals involving the **CIA** and contentious operations of the spy agency, 24/7 Wall St. poured over historical and media sources as well as declassified Senate, **CIA**, and other government ...

CIA chief in rare visit to Libya, meets Tripoli-based PM

3 days ago · TRIPOLI, Libya -- The **CIA** chief has met with one of Libya's rival prime ministers, the government in the country's capital of Tripoli said Thursday. It was a rare visit by a senior U.S. official ...

https://www.atlasobscura.com › articles › cia-cold-war-pigeon-spies

When the CIA Spied on American Citizens—Using Pigeons

4 days ago · Cher Ami, a black checker pigeon, earned his fame carrying messages for the American military during World War I. The pigeons recruited by the **CIA** during the Cold War were trained to undertake ...

https://www.theiia.org › en › certifications › cia

Certified Internal Auditor | Global Certification in Internal Audit ...

Prove Credibility & Proficiency. As the only globally recognized internal audit certification, becoming a Certified Internal Auditor ® (**CIA** ®) is the optimum way to communicate knowledge, skills, and competencies to effectively carry out professional responsibilities for any internal audit, anywhere in the world.. Earning a professional internal audit credential is a critical step to being ...

More Results

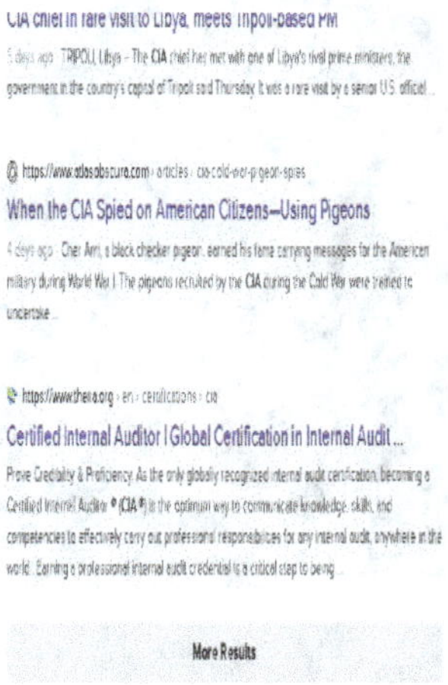

When the CIA Spied on American Citizens—Using Pigeons

4 days ago Cher Ami, a black checker pigeon, earned his fame carrying messages for the American military during World War I. The pigeons recruited by the **CIA** during the Cold War were trained to undertake ...

.....

Well… I *did* say pop culture.

…..

Heck with it, for this ubiquitous CIA stuff, I'm sticking with Wiki.

Now… about the video prep.

Yeah.

Well…

"It's time to invade…"

CIVIL WAR - Bay Of Pigs (Official Video) | Napalm Records
https://www.youtube.com/watch?v=lXAvNLTWNMM

(Napalm Records, 2015)

"... the profile of a CIA agent...foster kid...you know, that doesn't have any attachments to anybody..."

CIA Agents Explains What CIA Looks For in New Recruits
https://www.youtube.com/watch?v=SaFpr1VMfZQ

(Valuetainment Short Clips, 2021, 0:10)

"... I went to CIA headquarters to find out what they're looking for in new hires."

Want To Be A CIA Agent? Here's How To Become A Spy | CNBC
https://www.youtube.com/watch?v=h8FtstMvYH4

(CNBC, 2018, 0:19)

"... Kind of tell us as much as you can about what it's like. I mean is it like what you see in the movies?..."

CIA 101: Will explains what it's like to work undercover for the CIA

https://www.youtube.com/watch?v=ocMyoAOo3oA

(Beckcom, 2020, 0:20)

"...There are a lot of benefits in launching a coup d'état…"

A simple guide to overthrowing a nation (feat. the CIA)
https://www.youtube.com/watch?v=xDuMRAhe7Y0

(YEAH, I know he's asking for money, but he's also the most entertaining.)

(Tran, 2022, 0:09)

What the hell was I thinking when I put this together?

…..

I was thinking of a 13-year-old boy… with serious problems.

I was thinking of someone who is so thoroughly brainwashed… it just doesn't matter anymore.

Nothing ANYONE says or does matters at all… about ANYTHING.

I was thinking of someone who is NEVER affected by reality.

I was thinking of someone who is not only thoroughly brainwashed, but of someone who WANTS to be thoroughly brainwashed.

…..

I was also thinking about this:

"I seen another one of them double naught spy movies. Uncle Jed, that is what I was meant to be!..."

Double knot spy
https://www.youtube.com/watch?v=1MWq6L19eNo

(Excallibro, 2011, 0:25)

Irresponsible?

I should be more somber about all this?

…..

Yeah, well, this is called self-preservation.

And it's not just a question of still having to return to this country…

It's about just not allowing yourself to be driven insane.

…..

And yes, it is that simple.

…..

Perhaps not that easy, but yeah, that simple.

Complicate things if you want.

See how far that gets you.

Don't get me wrong, had reliable information that the general public could have processed been available, this would be a VERY different list.

….

But I'm also from Miami.

So, here's _my_ list:

"At a secret base in the Guatemalan jungle, American CIA agents have been training Cuban exiles to invade Cuba…"

Cuba & Bay Of Pigs
https://www.youtube.com/watch?v=8qXZp8bxpNY

(ColdWarWarriors, 2009)

"In April of 1962, anti-Castro Cuban exiles staged an invasion at Cuba's Bay of Pigs. The CIA, who was behind the 3-day operation, would come to consider it one of the most colossal blunders in their entire history…

"Everything That Went Wrong During the Bay of Pigs Invasion
https://www.youtube.com/watch?v=HIhQSjR3s3c

(Weird History, 2020)

"...Covertly funded by the CIA, the 3-day Bay of Pigs invasion
would prove to be a disaster for the Kennedy administration…"
Bay of Pigs Invasion
https://www.youtube.com/watch?v=Ld5MRuMJKWQ

(Daily Dose Documentary, 2020, 0:04)

"...I came to fight the mercenaries who come to attack the
country..."

Fidel Castro: Remembering the Bay of Pigs
https://www.youtube.com/watch?v=iT6msx5nVgk

(CBC News: The National, 2016, 0:45)

…..

Okay, here are a few more if you're interested:

"What happens in the 1990's is that the Cold War ends, and all of a sudden the CIA is left without a
visible, viable enemy to justify its existence. If they were going to continue, they had to do something to improve their public image…"

Covert operations: How the CIA works with Hollywood - Listening Post (Feature)
https://www.youtube.com/watch?v=kYYXnTdObKI&t=307s

(Al Jazeera English, 2017, 5:02)

"...they did not see that one coming..."

How The CIA Got Started - US 101
https://www.youtube.com/watch?v=UEG88if1K-4&t=560s

(US 101, 2018, 3:55)

"...putting out false stories into the world to cause confusion and distrust via radio, leaflets, and word-of-mouth against YOU, who, uhmm, in this instance are an enemy of America…"

101 Facts About The CIA
https://www.youtube.com/watch?v=Rw90MWARES8

(101Facts, 2017, 2:22)

Timeline – Part 2

All right, at this point, we're just going to jump into WWII:

1939

World War II

"World War II or the Second World War, often abbreviated as WWII or WW2, was a global conflict that lasted from 1939 to 1945. The vast majority of the world's countries, including all of the great powers, fought as part of two opposing military alliances: the Allies and the Axis. Many participants threw their economic, industrial, and scientific capabilities behind this total war, blurring the distinction between civilian and military resources. Aircraft played a major role, enabling the strategic bombing of population centres and the only two nuclear weapons ever used in war…"

("World War II," 2023)

1939

KKK

"… In 1939, after experiencing several years of decline due to the Great Depression, the Imperial Wizard Hiram Wesley Evans sold the national organization to James A. Colescott, an Indiana veterinary physician, and Samuel Green, an Atlanta obstetrician. They could not revive the Klan's declining membership…"

("Ku Klux Klan," 2023)

1941

World War II – U.S. Involvement – 1941 to 1945

("List of wars involving the United States," 2023)

CIA

"… The success of the British Commandos during World War II prompted U.S. President Franklin D. Roosevelt to authorize the creation of an intelligence service modeled after the British Secret Intelligence Service (MI6), and Special Operations Executive. This led to the creation of the Office of Strategic Services (OSS) established by a Presidential military order issued by President Roosevelt on June 13, 1942…"

("Central Intelligence Agency," 2023)

"… President Franklin D. Roosevelt established the Office of Strategic Services (OSS), the forerunner to today's CIA, and appointed New York lawyer and World War I hero General William J. Donovan to head the fledgling agency. The original mandate of the OSS was to collect and analyze "strategic information" for use in war…"

("CIA," 2018)

"… In June 1942 Roosevelt created the OSS to bring together the fragmented and uncoordinated strands of U.S. foreign intelligence gathering in a single organization…"

(Pringle, 2022)

1944

KKK

"… In 1944, the Internal Revenue Service filed a lien for $685,000 in back taxes against the Klan, and Colescott dissolved the organization that year. Local Klan groups closed down over the following years…"

("Ku Klux Klan," 2023)

"… the organization temporarily disbanded in 1944…"

("Ku Klux Klan," 2022)

1945

CIA

"… On September 20, 1945, shortly after the end of World War II, Harry S. Truman signed an executive order dissolving the OSS, and by October 1945 its functions had been divided between the

Departments of State and War. The division lasted only a few months. The first public mention of the "Central Intelligence Agency" appeared on a command-restructuring proposal presented by Jim Forrestal and Arthur Radford to the U.S. Senate Military Affairs Committee at the end of 1945…"

("Central Intelligence Agency," 2023)

"… Under Donovan's capable, if unorthodox, direction, the OSS was remarkably effective, despite the initial inexperience of most of its personnel. Its successes notwithstanding, the OSS was dismantled at the conclusion of the war…"

(Pringle, 2022)

"… At the conclusion of World War II, however, President Harry Truman, who had taken office following Roosevelt's death, didn't see a need for the OSS and abolished it. Within a year of that decision—and after the beginning of the Cold War between the United States and the Soviet Union—the new president had a change of heart…"

("CIA," 2018)

KKK

"… After World War II, the folklorist and author Stetson Kennedy infiltrated the Klan; he provided internal data to media and law enforcement agencies. He also provided secret code words to the writers of the Superman radio program, resulting in episodes in which Superman took on the KKK. Kennedy stripped away the Klan's mystique and trivialized its rituals and code words, which may have contributed to the decline in Klan recruiting and membership. In the 1950s Kennedy wrote a bestselling book about his experiences, which further damaged the Klan…"

("Ku Klux Klan," 2023)

1946

<u>CIA</u>

"… President Harry S. Truman had created the Central Intelligence Group under the direction of a Director of Central Intelligence by presidential directive on January 22, 1946, and this group was transformed into the Central Intelligence Agency by implementation of the National Security Act of 1947…"

("Central Intelligence Agency," 2023)

"… With many of the former OSS leaders still on hand in Washington, he first established a Central Intelligence Group and a National Intelligence Agency in 1946. Then, in 1947, Congress passed the National Security Act, which led to the formation of the National Security Council and the CIA as it's known today…"

("CIA," 2018)

"… In 1946 Pres. Harry S. Truman, recognizing the need for a coordinated postwar intelligence establishment, created by executive order a Central Intelligence Group and a National Intelligence Authority… In 1947 Congress passed the National Security Act, which created the National Security Council (NSC) and, under its direction, the CIA…"

(Pringle, 2022)

1950

Korean War

"… The Korean War (also known by other names) was fought between North Korea and South Korea from 1950 to 1953. The war began on 25 June 1950 when North Korea invaded South Korea following clashes along the border and rebellions in South Korea. North Korea was supported by China and the Soviet Union while South Korea was supported by the United States and allied countries. The fighting ended with an armistice on 27 July 1953…"

("Korean War," 2023)

1953

CIA

1953 Iranian coup d'état
"… Under CIA Director Allen Dulles, Operation Ajax was put into motion. Its goal was to overthrow Mossadegh with military support from General Fazlollah Zahedi and install a pro-western regime headed by the Shah of Iran…"

Early Cold War, 1953–1966
"… The CIA was involved in anti-Communist activities in
Burma, Congo, Guatemala, and Laos. Operations in Laos
continued well into the 1970s…"

("Central Intelligence Agency," 2023)

OH, HERE'S A FUN ONE, BOYS AND GIRLS…

Project MKUltra

*Project MKUltra (or MK-Ultra) was an illegal
human experimentation program designed and
undertaken by the U.S. Central Intelligence Agency
(CIA), intended to develop procedures and identify
drugs that could be used in interrogations to
weaken individuals and force confessions through
brainwashing and psychological torture. It began
in 1953 and was halted in 1973. MKUltra used
numerous methods to manipulate its subjects'
mental states and brain functions, such as the
covert administration of high doses of psychoactive
drugs (especially LSD) and other chemicals,
electroshocks, hypnosis, sensory deprivation,
isolation, and verbal and sexual abuse, in addition
to other forms of torture.*

*MKUltra was preceded by two drug-related
experiments, Project Bluebird and Project
Artichoke. It was organized through the CIA's*

Office of Scientific Intelligence and coordinated with the United States Army Biological Warfare Laboratories. The program engaged in illegal activities, including the use of U.S. and Canadian citizens as unwitting test subjects. Over 7,000 American veterans took part in these experiments non-consensually during the 1950s through 1970s, many of them suing later on. MKUltra's scope was broad, with activities carried out under the guise of research at more than 80 institutions aside from the military, including colleges and universities, hospitals, prisons, and pharmaceutical companies. The CIA operated using front organizations, although some top officials at these institutions were aware of the CIA's involvement.

MKUltra was first brought to public attention in 1975 by the Church Committee of the United States Congress and Gerald Ford's United States President's Commission on CIA activities within the United States (also known as the Rockefeller Commission). Investigative efforts were hampered by CIA Director Richard Helms's order that all MKUltra files be destroyed in 1973; the Church Committee and Rockefeller Commission investigations relied on the sworn testimony of direct participants and on the small number of documents that survived Helms's order. In 1977, a Freedom of Information Act request uncovered a cache of 20,000 documents relating to MKUltra, which led to Senate hearings. Some surviving information about MKUltra was declassified in July 2001.

("MKUltra," 2023)

1955

Vietnam War

"… The Vietnam War (also known by other names) was a conflict in Vietnam, Laos, and Cambodia from 1 November 1955 to the fall of Saigon on 30 April 1975. It was the second of the Indochina Wars and was officially fought between North Vietnam and South Vietnam. The north was supported by the Soviet Union, China, and other communist states, while the south was supported by the United States and other anti-communist allies. The war is widely considered to be a Cold War-era proxy war. It lasted almost 20 years, with direct U.S. involvement ending in 1973. The conflict also spilled over into neighboring states, exacerbating the Laotian Civil War and the Cambodian Civil War, which ended with all three countries becoming communist states by 1975…"

("Vietnam War," 2023)

1958

CIA

"… 'We had constructed for ourselves a picture of the USSR, and whatever happened had to be made to fit into this picture.

Intelligence estimators can hardly commit a more abominable sin.' On December 16, Eisenhower received a report from his intelligence board of consultants that said the agency was 'incapable of making objective appraisals of its own intelligence information as well as its own operations.'…"

Indochina, Tibet and the Vietnam War (1954–1975)
"… The CIA Tibetan program consisted of political plots, propaganda distribution, and paramilitary and intelligence gathering based on U.S. commitments made to the Dalai Lama in 1951 and 1956...Sometime between 1959 and 1961, the CIA started Project Tiger, a program of dropping South Vietnamese agents into North Vietnam to gather intelligence. These were failures; the Deputy Chief for Project Tiger, Captain Do Van Tien, admitted that he was an agent for Hanoi…"

("Central Intelligence Agency," 2023)

1958

Lebanon crisis (1958), Laotian Civil War (1959–1975) Part of the Indochina Wars and Cold War

("List of wars involving the United States," 2023)

1950's & 1960's

KKK

Among the more notorious murders by Klan members in the 1950s and 1960s:

The 1951 Christmas Eve bombing of the home of National Association for the Advancement of Colored People (NAACP) activists Harry and Harriette Moore in Mims, Florida, resulting in their deaths.

The 1957 murder of Willie Edwards Jr., who was forced by Klansmen to jump to his death from a bridge into the Alabama River.

The 1963 assassination of NAACP organizer Medgar Evers in Mississippi. In 1994, former Ku Klux Klansman Byron De La Beckwith was convicted.

The 16th Street Baptist Church bombing in September 1963 in Birmingham, Alabama, which killed four African-American girls and injured 22 people. The perpetrators were Klan members Robert Chambliss, convicted in 1977, Thomas Edwin Blanton Jr. and Bobby Frank Cherry, convicted in 2001 and 2002. The fourth suspect, Herman Cash, died before he was indicted.

The 1964 murders of Chaney, Goodman, and Schwerner, three civil rights workers, in Mississippi. In June 2005, Klan member Edgar Ray Killen was convicted of manslaughter.

The 1964 murder of two Black teenagers, Henry Hezekiah Dee and Charles Eddie Moore in Mississippi. In August 2007, based on the confession of Klansman Charles Marcus Edwards, James Ford Seale, a reputed Ku Klux Klansman, was convicted. Seale was sentenced to serve three life sentences. Seale was a former Mississippi policeman and sheriff's deputy.

The 1965 Alabama murder of Viola Liuzzo. She was a Southern-raised Detroit mother of five who was visiting the state in order to attend a civil rights march. At the time of her murder, Liuzzo was transporting Civil Rights marchers related to the Selma to Montgomery March.

The 1966 firebombing death of NAACP leader Vernon Dahmer Sr., 58, in Mississippi. In 1998 former Ku Klux Klan wizard Samuel Bowers was convicted of his murder and sentenced to life. Two other Klan members were indicted with Bowers, but one died before trial and the other's indictment was dismissed.

In July 1966, in Bogalusa, Louisiana, a stronghold of Klan activity, Clarence Triggs was found murdered.

The 1967 multiple bombings in Jackson, Mississippi, of the residence of a Methodist activist, Robert Kochtitzky, the synagogue, and the residence of Rabbi Perry Nussbaum. These were carried out by Klan member Thomas Albert Tarrants III, who was convicted in 1968. Another Klan bombing was averted in Meridian the same year.

("Ku Klux Klan," 2023)

Bay of Pigs

Bay of Pigs Invasion (1961) Part of the Cold War

("List of wars involving the United States," 2023)

BAY OF PIGS…

This one belongs to everyone from Miami.

"The Bay of Pigs Invasion (Spanish: Invasión de Bahía de Cochinos, sometimes called Invasión de Playa Girón or Batalla de Playa Girón after the Playa Girón) was a failed military landing operation on the southwestern coast of Cuba in 1961 by Cuban exiles, covertly financed and directed by the United States. It was aimed at overthrowing Fidel Castro's communist government. The operation took place at the height of the Cold War, and its failure influenced relations between Cuba, the United States, and the Soviet Union…"

("Bay of Pigs Invasion," 2023)

"Bay of Pigs invasion, (April 17, 1961), abortive invasion of Cuba at the Bahía de Cochinos (Bay of Pigs), or Playa Girón (Girón Beach) to Cubans, on the southwestern coast by some 1,500 Cuban exiles opposed to Fidel Castro. The invasion was financed and directed by the U.S. government…"

("Bay of Pigs invasion Cuban-United States history," 2023)

"The Bay of Pigs Invasion in 1961 was a failed attack launched by the CIA during the Kennedy administration to push Cuban leader Fidel Castro from power. Since 1959, officials at the U.S. State Department and the CIA had attempted to remove Castro. Finally, on April 17, 1961, the CIA launched what its leaders believed would be the definitive strike: a full-scale invasion of Cuba by 1,400 American-trained Cubans who had fled their homes when Castro took over. However, the invasion was doomed from the start. The invaders were badly outnumbered by Castro's troops, and they surrendered after less than 24 hours of fighting…"

("Bay of Pigs Invasion," 2022)

"Just off Florida's west coast near Fort Myers lies Useppa Island, now an exclusive seaside retreat for the wealthy. Sixty years ago, it was a very different place. In 1961 a small contingent of Cuban exiles, under the direction of the CIA, began training on the island for the military debacle that would become known as the Bay of Pigs invasion…"

(Simmons, 2021)

Yeah, I know I said I was just doing Wiki, but you know…

…..

Too much?

…..

Put together your own d### timeline!

1960's

<u>KKK</u>

"… The civil rights movement of the 1960s saw a surge of local Klan activity across the South, including the bombings, beatings and shootings of Black and white activists. These actions, carried out in secret but apparently the work of local Klansmen, outraged the nation and helped win support for the civil rights cause…"

("Ku Klux Klan," 2022)

1964

CIA

Brazil
"… The CIA and the United States government were involved in the 1964 Brazilian coup d'état. The coup occurred from March 31 to April 1, which resulted in the Brazilian Armed Forces ousting President João Goulart…"
("Central Intelligence Agency," 2023)

1966

Dominican Civil War (1965–1966), Korean DMZ Conflict (1966–1969) Part of the Korean conflict and the Cold War, Cambodian Civil War (1967–1975) Part of the Cold War

("List of wars involving the United States," 2023)

CIA

1967

"… in the fall of 1967, the CIA launched a domestic surveillance program code-named Chaos that would linger for a total of seven years. Police departments across the country cooperated in tandem with the agency, amassing a "computer index of 300,000 names of American people and organizations, and extensive files on 7,200 citizens." Helms hatched a 'Special Operations Group' in which '[eleven] CIA officers grew long hair, learned the jargon of the New Left, and went off to infiltrate peace groups in the United States and Europe.'…"

1971

"… On June 17, Nixon's **Plumbers** were caught burglarizing the DNC offices in the Watergate…" (Five former CIA officers that broke in to wire-tap the joint… Just in case you've been living under a rock, or something.)

("Central Intelligence Agency," 2023)

1979

KKK

"… On November 3, 1979, five communist protesters were killed by KKK and American Nazi Party members in Greensboro, North Carolina, in what is known as the Greensboro massacre…"

("Ku Klux Klan," 2023)

<u>*CIA*</u>

1980's

Chad
"… Chad's neighbor Libya was a major source of weaponry to communist rebel forces. The CIA seized the opportunity to arm and finance Chad's Prime Minister, Hissène Habré, after he created a breakaway government in western Sudan, even giving him Stinger missiles…"

Afghanistan
"… In Afghanistan, the CIA funneled several billion dollars worth of weapons, including FIM-92 Stinger surface-to-air missiles, to Pakistani Inter-Services Intelligence (ISI), which funneled them to tens of thousands of Afghan mujahideen resistance fighters—a portion of which bled to foreign "Afghan Arabs" from forty Muslim countries. In total, the CIA sent approximately 2,300 Stingers to Afghanistan, creating a substantial black market for the weapons throughout the Middle East, Central Asia, and even parts of Africa that persisted well into the 1990s…"

1981

Iran/Contra
"… The CIA was arming and training Nicaraguans Contras in Honduras in hopes that they could depose the Sandinistas in Nicaragua…"

("Central Intelligence Agency," 2023)

1982

Multinational intervention in Lebanon (1982–1984)

("List of wars involving the United States," 2023)

1983

CIA

Lebanon
"… On April 18, 1983, a 2,000 lb car bomb exploded in the lobby
of the American embassy in Beirut, killing 63 people, including
17 Americans and 7 CIA officers, including Robert Ames, one of
the CIA's Middle East experts. America's fortunes in Lebanon
suffered more as America's poorly-directed retaliation for the
bombing was interpreted by many as support for the Maronite
minority. On October 23, 1983, two bombs (1983 Beirut
Bombing) were set off in Beirut, including a 10-ton bomb at a US
military barracks that killed 242 people. – The Embassy bombing
killed the CIA's Beirut Station Chief, Ken Haas. Bill Buckley was
sent in to replace him. Eighteen days after the US Marines left
Lebanon, Buckley was kidnapped. On March 7, 1984, Jeremy
Levin, CNN Bureau Chief in Beirut, was kidnapped. Twelve more
Americans were captured in Beirut during the Reagan
Administration…"

("Central Intelligence Agency," 2023)

1983

United States invasion of Grenada (1983) Part of the Cold War, Bombing of Libya (1986), Tanker War (1987–1988), United States invasion of Panama (1989–1990)

("List of wars involving the United States," 2023)

1990

Gulf War

"… The Gulf War was a 1990–1991 armed campaign waged by a 35-country military coalition in response to the Iraqi invasion of Kuwait. Spearheaded by the United States, the coalition's efforts against Iraq were carried out in two key phases: Operation Desert Shield, which marked the military buildup from August 1990 to January 1991; and Operation Desert Storm, which began with the aerial bombing campaign against Iraq on 17 January 1991 and came to a close with the American-led Liberation of Kuwait on 28 February 1991…"

("Gulf War," 2023)

<u>*1991*</u>

Iraqi No-Fly Zone Enforcement Operations (1991–2003)

("List of wars involving the United States," 2023)

1991

<u>*KKK*</u>

"… In 1991 former Ku Klux Klan grand wizard David Duke ran for governor of Louisiana and finished ahead of incumbent Gov. Buddy Roemer in the gubernatorial primary election, a stunning upset that garnered international attention. The possibility that a former grand wizard might be elected governor created a media firestorm and made the 1991 Louisiana gubernatorial election the most closely watched in the country. Duke's campaign lost steam when advocacy groups such as the National Association for the Advancement of Colored People (NAACP) and major corporations threatened to respond to a Duke victory by mounting an economic boycott of Louisiana, whose economy depended on tourism. As a result. former governor Edwin Edwards defeated Duke by a margin of 61 percent to 39 percent, though Duke won slightly over 50 percent of the white vote…"

(Wallenfeldt, n.d.)

1991

CIA

Fall of the USSR
"… All the CIA numbers on the USSR's economy were wrong.
Too often the CIA relied on inexperienced people supposedly
deemed experts. Bob Gates had preceded Doug MacEachin as
Chief of Soviet analysis, and he had never visited Russia. Few
officers, even those stationed in the country, spoke the language
of the people on whom they spied… The CIA analysis of Russia
during the Cold War was either driven by ideology, or by
politics…"

("Central Intelligence Agency," 2023)

_1992_

First U.S. Intervention in the Somali Civil War (1992–1995) Part
of the Somali civil war (1991–present), Bosnian War and Croatian
War (1992–1995) Part of the Yugoslav Wars, Intervention in Haiti
(1994–1995)

("List of wars involving the United States," 2023)

<u>*CIA*</u>

1993

"… On January 25, 1993, Mir Qazi opened fire at the CIA headquarters in Langley, Virginia, killing two officers and wounding three others…"

1997

"… CIA officers know little about the language or politics of the people they spy on; the conclusion was that the CIA lacked the 'depth, breadth, and expertise to monitor political, military, and economic developments worldwide.'… 'intelligence failure is inevitable'…"

"… Between 1991 and 1998 the CIA lost 3,000 employees…"

("Central Intelligence Agency," 2023)

1997

<u>*KKK*</u>

Henry Francis Hays was executed in Alabama for the death of Michael Donald on June 6, 1997. It was the first time since 1913 that a white man had been executed in Alabama for a crime against an African American.

("Ku Klux Klan," 2023)

_**1998**_

Kosovo War (1998–1999) Part of the Yugoslav Wars

("List of wars involving the United States," 2023)

21st-Century

CIA

"… In 2000, the CIA and USAF jointly ran a series of flights over Afghanistan with a small remote-controlled reconnaissance drone, the Predator; they obtained probable photos of bin Laden. Cofer Black and others became advocates of arming the Predator with missiles to try to assassinate bin Laden and other al-Qaeda leaders. After the Cabinet-level Principals Committee meeting on terrorism of September 4, 2001, the CIA resumed reconnaissance flights, the drones now being weapons-capable…"

("Central Intelligence Agency," 2023)

2001

War in Afghanistan

"… The War in Afghanistan was an armed conflict from 2001 to 2021. It began when an international military coalition led by the United States launched an invasion of Afghanistan, toppling the Taliban-ruled Islamic Emirate and establishing the internationally recognized Islamic Republic three years later. The conflict ultimately ended with the 2021 Taliban offensive, which overthrew the Islamic Republic, and re-established the Islamic Emirate. It was the longest war in the military history of the United States, surpassing the length of the Vietnam War (1955–1975) by approximately 6 months…"

("War in Afghanistan [2001–2021]," 2023)

2001

CIA

CIA field office destroyed during the attack on the World Trade Center.

"… The involvement of the CIA in the newly coined "War on Terror" was further increased on September 15, 2001…"

"… On November 25–27, 2001, Taliban prisoners revolted at the Qala Jangi prison west of Mazar-e-Sharif. Though several days of struggle occurred between the Taliban prisoners and the Northern Alliance members present, the prisoners gained the upper hand and obtained North Alliance weapons. At some point during this period Johnny "Mike" Spann, a CIA officer sent to question the prisoners, was beaten to death. He became the first American to die in combat in the war in Afghanistan…"

("Central Intelligence Agency," 2023)

2002

American intervention in Yemen (2002–present) Part of the War on terror, the Al-Qaeda insurgency in Yemen, the Yemeni Civil War and the Saudi Arabian-led intervention in Yemen

("List of wars involving the United States," 2023)

2003

Iraq War

The Iraq War was a protracted armed conflict in Iraq from 2003 to 2011 that began with the invasion of Iraq by the United States-led coalition that overthrew the Iraqi government of Saddam Hussein. The conflict continued for much of the next decade as an insurgency emerged to oppose the coalition forces and the post-invasion Iraqi government. US troops were officially withdrawn in 2011. The United States became re-involved in 2014 at the head of a new coalition, and the insurgency and many dimensions of the armed conflict continue today. The invasion occurred as part of the George W. Bush administration's War on terror following the September 11 attacks, despite no connection between Iraq and the attacks.

("Iraq War," 2023)

2003

CIA

Iraq War
"… A postmortem of the intelligence failures in the lead up to Iraq led by former DDCI Richard Kerr would conclude that the CIA had been a casualty of the Cold War, wiped out in a way 'analogous to the effect of the meteor strikes on the dinosaurs.' – The opening days of the invasion of Iraq would see successes and defeats for the CIA. With its Iraq networks compromised, and its strategic and tactical information shallow, and often wrong, the intelligence side of the invasion itself would be a black eye for the agency…"

("Central Intelligence Agency," 2023)

2004

American intervention in the War in North-West Pakistan (2004–2018) Part of the War on terror and the War in North-West

Pakistan, Second U.S. Intervention in the Somali Civil War
(2007–present) Part of the Somali Civil War, the Somali Civil
War and the War on terror, Operation Ocean Shield (2009–2016)
Part of the War on terror, International intervention in Libya
(2011) Part of the Libyan Crisis and the First Libyan Civil War,
Operation Observant Compass (2011–2017) Part of the War on
terror and the Lord's Resistance Army insurgency

("List of wars involving the United States," 2023)

<u>*CIA*</u>

2011

Operation Neptune Spear
"… On May 1, 2011, President Barack Obama announced that
Osama bin Laden was killed earlier that day by "a small team of
Americans" operating in Abbottabad, Pakistan, during a CIA
operation. The raid was executed from a CIA forward base in
Afghanistan by elements of the U.S. Navy's Naval Special
Warfare Development Group and CIA paramilitary operatives…"

2011

"… Anwar al-Awlaki, a Yemeni-American U.S. citizen and al-
Qaeda member, was killed on September 30, 2011, by an airstrike
conducted by the Joint Special Operations Command. After
several days of surveillance of Awlaki by the Central Intelligence
Agency, armed drones took off from a new, secret American base
in the Arabian Peninsula, crossed into northern Yemen, and fired
several Hellfire missiles at al-Awlaki's vehicle. Samir Khan, a
Pakistani-American al-Qaeda member and editor of the jihadist
Inspire magazine, also reportedly died in the attack. The
combined CIA/JSOC drone strike was the first in Yemen since

2002 – there have been others by the military's Special Operations forces – and was part of an effort by the spy agency to duplicate in Yemen the covert war which has been running in Afghanistan and Pakistan…"

2012

Syrian Civil War
"… Under the aegis of operation Timber Sycamore and other clandestine activities, CIA operatives and U.S. special operations troops have trained and armed nearly 10,000 rebel fighters at a cost of $1 billion a year. The CIA has been sending weapons to anti-government rebels in Syria since at least 2012…"

("Central Intelligence Agency," 2023)

I've already mentioned how compelling I found Wiki's war list. - This is the part that clinched it… It just made so much sense.

2014

American-led intervention in Iraq (2014–2021) *Part of the Operation Inherent Resolve, the War in Iraq (2013–2017), the Spillover of the Syrian civil war, the War on terror and the International ISIS campaign,* American-led intervention in Syria (2014–present) *Part of the Operation Inherent Resolve, the Syrian civil war, the War on terror and the International ISIS campaign,* American intervention in Libya (2015–2019) *Part of the Operation Inherent Resolve, the Second Libyan Civil War, the War on terror, and the International ISIS Campaign*

("List of wars involving the United States," 2023)

Wrapping It Up

"… The cases of Klan-related violence became more isolated in the decades to come, though fragmented groups became aligned with neo-Nazi or other right-wing extremist organizations from the 1970s onward.

As of 2016, the Anti-Defamation League estimated Klan membership to be around 3,000, while the Southern Poverty Law Center said there were 6,000 members total."

("Ku Klux Klan," 2022)

"…Despite the persistence of racism, the Klan largely failed to stem the growth of racial tolerance in the South in the late 20th century. Though the organization continued some of its surreptitious activities into the early 21st century, cases of Klan violence became more isolated, and its membership had declined to a few thousand. The Klan became a chronically fragmented mélange made up of several separate and competing groups, some of which occasionally entered into alliances with neo-Nazi and other right-wing extremist groups, as was the case at a demonstration in Charlottesville, Virginia, in August 2017 that erupted in violence, resulting in the death of a counterdemonstrator."

(Wallenfeldt, n.d.)

"… The modern KKK is not one organization; rather it is composed of small independent chapters across the United States. According to a 1999 ADL report, the KKK's estimated size then was 'No more than a few thousand, organized into slightly more than 100 units'. In 2017, the Southern Poverty Law Center (SPLC), which monitors extremist groups, estimated that there were 'at least 29 separate, rival Klan groups currently active in the United States, and they compete with one another for members, dues, news media attention and the title of being the true heir to the Ku Klux Klan'… A 2016 analysis by the SPLC found that hate groups in general were on the rise in the United States. The ADL published a report in 2016 that concluded: 'Despite a persistent ability to attract media attention, organized Ku Klux Klan groups are actually continuing a long-term trend of decline. They remain a collection of mostly small, disjointed groups that continually change in name and leadership.'…"

("Ku Klux Klan," 2023)

The CIA today?

…..

Freedom fighters! – Totally dedicated to freedom.

…..

Pretty good place to work.

….

Oh, and I hear there's a new Morgan Freeman movie about them… *yeah, uh-huh!*

…..

Brian Berletic
"Unfortunately, here in Bangkok, I wouldn't touch the expat community with a 10-foot pole...
These are the people that get involved in politics because they have this resentment. They just
want to see everything trashed. There's some real pathology here…"

The Roundtable #37: The Expat Experience with Alex Christoforou and Brian Berletic
https://www.youtube.com/watch?v=84SGzC5nCX0

(Lira, 2022, 35:55)

…..

"… The organization took as its symbol a burning cross and held rallies, parades and marches around the country. At its peak in the 1920s, Klan membership exceeded 4 million people nationwide…"

History.com - Ku Klux Klan (online article)
https://www.history.com/topics/reconstruction/ku-klux-klan

("Ku Klux Klan," 2022)

…..

You think *CIA* membership will ever exceed 4 million people nationwide?

References

101Facts. (2017, March 10). *101 Facts About The CIA*. [Video]. YouTube. https://www.youtube.com/watch?v=Rw90MWARES8

Al Jazeera English. (2017, October 22). *Covert operations: How the CIA works with Hollywood - Listening Post (Feature)*. [Video]. YouTube. https://www.youtube.com/watch?v=kYYXnTdObKI&t=307s

American Civil War. (2023, January 20). In *Wikipedia.* https://en.wikipedia.org/wiki/American_Civil_War

Baumruk, T. (2012, July 9). *Roy Clark - Do You Believe This Town.* [Video]. YouTube. https://www.youtube.com/watch?v=C0ceQumLxYY

Bay of Pigs Invasion. (2022, November 9). In *History.com.* https://www.history.com/topics/cold-war/bay-of-pigs-invasion

Bay of Pigs Invasion. (2023, January 17). In Wikipedia. https://en.wikipedia.org/wiki/Bay_of_Pigs_Invasion

Bay of Pigs invasion Cuban-United States history. (2023, January 6). In *Encyclopædia Britannica.* https://www.britannica.com/event/Bay-of-Pigs-invasion

Beckcom, B. (2020, August 4). *CIA 101: Will explains what it's like to work undercover for the CIA.* [Video]. YouTube. https://www.youtube.com/watch?v=ocMyoAOo3oA

CBC News: The National. (2016, March 21). *Fidel Castro: Remembering the Bay of Pigs*. [Video]. YouTube. https://www.youtube.com/watch?v=iT6msx5nVgk

Central Intelligence Agency. (2023, January 18). In *Wikipedia*. https://en.wikipedia.org/wiki/Central_Intelligence_Agency

CIA. (2018, August 21). In *History.com*. https://www.history.com/topics/us-government/history-of-the-cia

CNBC. (2018, April 6). *Want To Be A CIA Agent? Here's How To Become A Spy | CNBC*. [Video]. YouTube. https://www.youtube.com/watch?v=h8FtstMvYH4

ColdWarWarriors. (2009, February 1). *Cuba & Bay Of Pigs*. [Video]. YouTube. https://www.youtube.com/watch?v=8qXZp8bxpNY

Daily Dose Documentary. (2020, July 21). *Bay of Pigs Invasion*. [Video]. YouTube. https://www.youtube.com/watch?v=Ld5MRuMJKWQ

Doc Holiday. (2022, October 29). *Mississippi Burning 1988 part 9 (Full Movie)*. [Video]. YouTube. https://www.youtube.com/watch?v=plH2xKFKapE

Excallibro. (2011, February 8). *Double knot spy*. [Video]. YouTube. https://www.youtube.com/watch?v=1MWq6L19eNo

FoundationINTERVIEWS. (2016, July 13). *Phil Donahue on interviewing David Duke -EMMYTVLEGENDS.ORG*. [Video]. YouTube. https://www.youtube.com/watch?v=AnRjtg37two

Gulf War. (2023, January 16). In *Wikipedia*.
    https://en.wikipedia.org/wiki/Gulf_War

Hoffman, D. (2018, March 19). *His Smile Is Fake. Watch
    Southerners Tell Him Segregation Was Better For Black
    Americans.* [Video]. YouTube.
    https://www.youtube.com/watch?v=6gX6WIEzB08

Iraq War. (2023, January 18). In *Wikipedia*.
    https://en.wikipedia.org/wiki/Iraq_War

KKK founded. (2019, February 25). In *History.com*.
    https://www.history.com/this-day-in-history/kkk-founded

Korean War. (2023, January 16). In *Wikipedia*.
    https://en.wikipedia.org/wiki/Korean_War

Ku Klux Klan. (2022, February 4). In *History.com*.
    https://www.history.com/topics/reconstruction/ku-klux-
    klan

Ku Klux Klan. (2023, January 12). In *Wikipedia*.
https://en.wikipedia.org/wiki/Ku_Klux_Klan

Lira, G. [The Roundtable]. (2022, December 6). *The Roundtable
    #37: The Expat Experience with Alex Christoforou and
    Brian Berletic.* [Video]. YouTube.
    https://www.youtube.com/watch?v=84SGzC5nCX0

List of wars involving the United States. (2023, January 18). In
    Wikipedia.
    https://en.wikipedia.org/wiki/List_of_wars_involving_the
    _United_States

MKUltra. (2023, January 16). In *Wikipedia*.
https://en.wikipedia.org/wiki/MKUltra

Napalm Records. (2015, April 9). *CIVIL WAR - Bay Of Pigs (Official Video) | Napalm Records*. [Video]. YouTube. https://www.youtube.com/watch?v=lXAvNLTWNMM

OWN. (2015, January 2). *Oprah Visits a County Where No Black Person Had Lived for 75 Years | The Oprah Winfrey Show | OWN*. [Video]. YouTube. https://www.youtube.com/watch?v=WErjPmFulQ0

princetonacademics. (2014, May 28). *Segregation and the South - Fund for the Republic Records*. [Video]. YouTube. https://www.youtube.com/watch?v=tfgQdCld3Fg

Pringle, R. (2022, December 12). Central Intelligence Agency United States government. In *Encyclopædia Britannica.* https://www.britannica.com/topic/Central-Intelligence-Agency

Simmons, D.A. (2021, April 19). The fiasco at Cuba's Bay of Pigs. In *National Geographic.* https://www.nationalgeographic.com/newsletters/article/the-fiasco-at-cubas-bay-of-pigs-20210419

Spanish–American War. (2023, January 22). In *Wikipedia.* https://en.wikipedia.org/wiki/Spanish-American_War

TastySpaceApple. (2014, December 15). *George Wallace "Segregation Forever" Speech*. [Video]. YouTube. https://www.youtube.com/watch?v=6C-kBVggFrs

The Citadel. (2019, August 19). *Rite of Passage | Our Mighty Citadel*. [Video]. YouTube. https://www.youtube.com/watch?v=YYCgPCsnowc

The Ku Klux Klan | National Geographic Society. (2022, June 2). In *National Geographic.* https://education.nationalgeographic.org/resource/ku-klux-klan

The Norman Lear Effect. (2022, November 15). *The Jeffersons | Sorry, Wrong Meeting | Season 7 Episode 14 Full Episode | The Norman Lear Effect.* [Video]. YouTube. https://www.youtube.com/watch?v=cP-Fs2EashA

Tran, J. (2022, January 26). *A simple guide to overthrowing a nation (feat. the CIA).* [Video]. YouTube. https://www.youtube.com/watch?v=xDuMRAhe7Y0

TV Rerun Club by MGM. (2022, May 13). *300 Feet Below | Full Episode S01E01 | Flipper.* [Video]. YouTube. https://www.youtube.com/watch?v=cuKslEBQdSg

US 101. (2018, April 3). *How The CIA Got Started - US 101.* [Video]. YouTube. https://www.youtube.com/watch?v=UEG88if1K-4&t=560s

Valuetainment Short Clips. (2021, May 31). *CIA Agents Explains What CIA Looks For in New Recruits.* [Video]. YouTube. https://www.youtube.com/watch?v=SaFpr1VMfZQ

Vietnam War. (2023, January 10). In *Wikipedia.* https://en.wikipedia.org/wiki/Vietnam_War

Wallenfeldt, J. (n.d.). Revival of the Ku Klux Klan. In *Encyclopædia Britannica.* https://www.britannica.com/topic/Ku-Klux-Klan/Revival-of-the-Ku-Klux-Klan

War in Afghanistan (2001–2021). (2023, January 17). In *Wikipedia.* https://en.wikipedia.org/wiki/War_in_Afghanistan_(2001–2021)

Weird History. (2020, January 22). *Everything That Went Wrong During the Bay of Pigs Invasion.* [Video]. YouTube. https://www.youtube.com/watch?v=HIhQSjR3s3c

White, M. G. (n.d.). *American Wars Timeline: Major Wars Involving the US*. YourDictionary.com. https://examples.yourdictionary.com/american-wars-timeline-major-wars-involving-us.

World War I. (2023, January 22). In *Wikipedia*. https://en.wikipedia.org/wiki/World_War_I

World War II. (2023, January 17). In *Wikipedia*. https://en.wikipedia.org/wiki/World_War_II

www.ingramcontent.com/pod-product-compliance
Lightning Source LLC
Chambersburg PA
CBHW061513250726
48657CB00005B/1844